Africa's Animal GIANTS

by Jane R. McCauley

A male lion stays alert while drinking.

BOOKS FOR YOUNG EXPLORERS
NATIONAL GEOGRAPHIC SOCIETY

Far away in Africa, elephants stop at a water hole to drink and to bathe. They are thirsty and dusty, because they have come a long way. Dark clouds in the sky will bring rain. But most of the time, it is dry and hot on these flat plains.

Water is often hard to find for the elephants and the other animals living here. They sometimes go for days without a drink. Wherever there is a water hole, many kinds of animals must share it.

Like animals in a parade,
elephants follow each other
across the open plain. Elephants
travel together in herds,
looking for water and for roots,
leaves, and grass to eat.
Elephants are the largest of all
land animals. They really do not
have enemies, except for people
who hunt them for their tusks.

There are only a few trees here
to give shade. While walking
in the sun, the elephants swish
their big ears back and forth
like fans to help them stay cool.

An elephant's nose is a long trunk. The elephant uses its trunk to break off twigs and leaves to eat. The trunk is useful in many ways.

Wet and slippery, a baby elephant tries to climb up a riverbank. Its mother and an older sister help the baby with their trunks.

Another elephant
squirts water
into its mouth. Oops!
Some dribbles out.
The elephant
sucked the water up
with its trunk from
a hole in the ground.

7

An elephant chases a male lion away. Elephants don't hunt other animals for food. But if an animal comes too close, an elephant may charge. The elephant tucks its trunk under and spreads its ears out. It can run fast for a short distance.

Unlike elephants, lions hunt for meat to eat. Lions are the largest cats in Africa. The shaggy mane of the male makes him easy to spot. This hungry male growls and waits.

A lioness moves swiftly toward a herd of zebras.
Female lions catch most of the food for their family
groups, called prides. Together, the adults in a pride
may chase a whole herd of animals. If a lion is
hungry enough, it will even hunt alone.

Sleepy lions snooze in the branches of a tree. It is cooler than on the ground, and there are fewer pesky insects. Lions sleep for many hours a day. While she rests, a lioness keeps her cub close by to protect it.

Ostriches will not go to the water hole until the lions leave. By staying back, the ostriches can have a head start if one of the lions chases after them.

Ostriches can run so fast on their long legs that they rarely get caught. Ostriches are the largest of all birds. They have wings, but they cannot fly. The male can make a sound like a lion's roar when he opens his mouth wide. Baby ostriches grow quickly. In six months, the chicks walking beside their father may be taller than a man.

The rhinoceros is the only African giant with horns on its nose.
It uses the horns to protect itself and its young. The female
keeps her baby nearby until it can care for itself. By then,
the two bumps on the baby's nose will have grown into horns.
The main enemies of rhinos are people who hunt them for the horns.

Splash! A huge hippopotamus jumps into a river.
This animal is so heavy it sinks easily to the rocky bottom.

It walks along underwater, often following paths already
made by other hippos. The hippo is a good swimmer.
Soon it will swim to the surface and poke its head out
for air. Hippos spend most of the day in the water.

When a hippo is hungry, it climbs
out of the water to find grass.
The hippo looks big and clumsy, but
it has no trouble getting up the bank.
Many insects fly around the hippo.
Egrets and other birds wait
to snatch up the insects.

A baby hippo, only a few months old,
isn't even as big as its mother's head.
Her whiskers may tickle the little
hippo as she nuzzles it.

Are those big gray rocks in the river? Look closely, and you'll soon see that the "rocks" are really a herd of muddy hippos.

They stay cool by covering themselves with mud.
The mud helps keep their skin from drying out in the sun.

Mud also helps the Cape buffalo. A coating of mud on its skin keeps insects away. To lie down in the cool mud, the buffalo first lowers its head. Then it rolls on its side and back. Birds called oxpeckers pick ticks and flies off the buffalo's hide.

Riding on the big animal's back, an egret watches for insects. The buffalo stirs them up as it moves through the grass. In this way, the Cape buffalo and the birds are helping each other.

Giraffes are the tallest of all animals, even taller than many trees. To drink, giraffes spread their long front legs and lower their heads to the water. While drinking, they cannot watch for enemies. Often, one giraffe stands guard.

For a giraffe, eating is easier than drinking. To eat, it sticks out its long tongue and strips leaves off the trees. Most thorns won't hurt its tough lips.

Giraffes live in small herds, usually on the open plains. Because they are tall and have good eyesight, they can see enemies far away. Giraffes in a herd can watch in all directions. To find food, they head toward the trees that grow on the grassy plains. Some go even farther, into the hills near high mountains.

On shady forests high in the mountains, hairy gorillas make their homes. A playful young gorilla hangs upside down from a tree limb. It holds on tightly with its strong hands. Largest of all apes, the gorilla is really gentle and shy. It eats plants, and it rests a lot.

Whether deep in the forests or out on the plains, only in Africa do so many animal giants have a home in the wild.

PUBLISHED BY
The National Geographic Society, Washington, D. C.
Gilbert M. Grosvenor, PRESIDENT AND CHAIRMAN OF THE BOARD
Melvin M. Payne, CHAIRMAN EMERITUS
Owen R. Anderson, EXECUTIVE VICE PRESIDENT
Robert L. Breeden, SENIOR VICE PRESIDENT, PUBLICATIONS AND EDUCATIONAL MEDIA

PREPARED BY
The Special Publications and School Services Division
Donald J. Crump, DIRECTOR
Philip B. Silcott, ASSOCIATE DIRECTOR
Bonnie S. Lawrence, ASSISTANT DIRECTOR

STAFF FOR THIS BOOK
Jane H. Buxton, MANAGING EDITOR
Karen G. Yee, ILLUSTRATIONS EDITOR
Cinda Rose, ART DIRECTOR
Barbara A. Payne, RESEARCHER
Artemis S. Lampathakis, ILLUSTRATIONS ASSISTANT
Leslie Carol, Mary Elizabeth Ellison, Rosamund Garner, Sandra F. Lotterman, Eliza C. Morton,
  Valerie A. Woods, STAFF ASSISTANTS

ENGRAVING, PRINTING, AND PRODUCT MANUFACTURE
Robert W. Messer, MANAGER
George V. White, ASSISTANT MANAGER
David V. Showers, PRODUCTION MANAGER
George J. Zeller, Jr., PRODUCTION PROJECT MANAGER
Gregory Storer, SENIOR ASSISTANT PRODUCTION MANAGER; Mark R. Dunlevy, ASSISTANT PRODUCTION MANAGER;
  Timothy H. Ewing, PRODUCTION ASSISTANT; Carol R. Curtis, SENIOR PRODUCTION STAFF ASSISTANT

CONSULTANTS
William A. Xanten, Office of Animal Programs, National Zoological Park, Smithsonian Institution, SCIENTIFIC CONSULTANT
Dr. Ine Noe, EDUCATIONAL CONSULTANT
Dr. Lynda Bush, READING CONSULTANT

ILLUSTRATIONS CREDITS
Leonard Lee Rue III (Cover, 20-21, 22-23); Anthony Bannister (1); Jen and Des Bartlett (2-3, 4-5); Jen and Des Bartlett/ Bruce
Coleman Ltd. (6 upper); Rick Weyerhaeuser (6-7); Lee Lyon/Bruce Coleman Ltd. (7 right); Premaphotos Wildlife/K. G. Preston-
Mafham (8-9); K. & K. Ammann/Bruce Coleman Inc. (10 left); Stephen J. Krasemann/DRK PHOTO (10-11); Craig Packer/Bruce
Coleman Inc. (12); Arthus-Bertrand/Peter Arnold, Inc. (13 upper); Carol Hughes/Bruce Coleman Ltd. (13 lower); Jen and Des
Bartlett/Bruce Coleman Inc. (14 upper); Don W. Fawcett (14 left); John H. Hoffman/Bruce Coleman Inc. (14-15); Mohamed
Amin/Bruce Coleman Inc. (16); N. Myers/Bruce Coleman Inc. (17); Robert Caputo (18-19 upper); Alan Root/OKAPIA/Photo
Researchers (19 lower); K. & K. Ammann (21 right); Charles G. Summers, Jr. (24 upper, 24 lower right); Rita Summers (24 lower
left); Frans Lanting (25); Clem Haagner/Bruce Coleman Inc. (26-27); Günter Ziesler/Bruce Coleman Ltd. (27); Erwin and Peggy
Bauer/Bruce Coleman Inc. (28-29); Robert Campbell (30 left, 30-31); Jean-Loup Blanchet/PITCH (32).

Library of Congress CIP Data
McCauley, Jane R., 1947-
  Africa's animal giants.

  (Books for young explorers)
  Bibliography: p.
  Summary: Introduces the physical characteristics and habits of some of the largest animals
native to Africa, including the elephant, giraffe, hippopotamus, rhinoceros, gorilla, Cape
buffalo, lion, and ostrich.
  1. Zoology — Africa — Miscellanea — Juvenile literature. 2. Mammals — Africa —
Miscellanea — Juvenile literature. 3. Mammals — Africa — Size — Juvenile literature. [1.
Zoology — Africa. 2. Animals — Africa — Size] I. Title. II. Series.
QL336.M39 1987   599'.096   87-18488
ISBN 0-87044-680-0 (regular edition)   ISBN 0-87044-685-1 (library edition)

Cover: "Unk!" A hippo lifts its huge head from a watery bed of Nile lettuce. Hippos like to snack on these plants, which grow on the surface of rivers.

Below: Tall as a tower, a giraffe stands quietly alone at dusk.

MORE ABOUT AFRICA'S ANIMAL GIANTS

On the continent of Africa, visitors can see some of the biggest, fastest, and tallest animals on earth. The ancestors of these creatures once thrived in many parts of the world, but today most animal giants survive in the wild only in Africa. Different kinds of elephants, rhinos, buffaloes, and lions are also found on the continent of Asia.

Even in Africa, populations of most of the animals shown in this book are dwindling. As more land is cleared for farms and ranches, it is increasingly difficult for the animals to find enough living space, food, or water. Illegal hunting for tusks and horns has destroyed thousands of animals each year. Some animals have been relocated in national parks and reserves to help their species survive.

One of the most endangered of all the African giants is the mountain gorilla (30).* Gorillas, the largest of the apes, stay together in family groups. The leader of the group, which numbers about ten, is a silverback. Named for the swatch of gray across his back, he is often the largest and oldest male. The leader decides when the group will move on and selects nesting and feeding sites. By living together, gorillas can better protect their young, which may remain dependent for as long as ten years.

The rhinoceros is another of the most endangered African giants. Unlike gorillas, however, rhinos are generally solitary creatures. Of the five species of rhinos, only the black (16-17) and the white live in Africa. Both species are actually gray in color. They range across the open plains into the dense forests.

A baby rhino rarely leaves its mother's side until she has another calf, in about three to four years. When an enemy approaches, the female rhino charges, then attempts to butt or hook it with her two horns. The horns may fall off if they hit an object hard enough. But over time the horns regenerate. Since the 1800s, hunters have killed rhinos for their horns, which are believed by some to have magical and curative powers. The horns are also used to make dagger handles that are highly prized by some people.

Elephant (2-9) populations have also declined due to poaching. Their ivory tusks are used to make decorative objects. The tusks may

A family of mountain gorillas troops across a forest clearing to a new feeding spot. The patch of silvery hair across his back identifies the silverback, the leader of the group. A young gorilla rides on its mother's shoulders. Every day, the gorillas move around in search of food, making leafy nests to sleep in at night.

*Numbers in parentheses refer to pages in *Africa's Animal Giants*.

PETER VEIT

reach several feet in length as they continue to grow throughout the elephant's life. But sometimes the tusks break off while the elephant is fighting or is prying the bark off trees.

An elephant herd is a closely knit group. Related females and their offspring make up a herd; adult males usually live alone or with other males. The females cooperate in caring for the young. This includes keeping close watch on sick or injured babies. A female elephant gives birth every two to four years, after a 22-month pregnancy—the longest of any mammal.

Elephants have dexterous trunks, which they use to do a variety of things, such as plucking berries from bushes and helping their calves along. They breathe through two nostrils at the tip of the trunk. The two species of elephants—the one in Asia and the one in Africa—have trunks that look somewhat alike. But the ears of the African elephant are much larger than those of the Asian.

On Africa's grasslands, or savannas, the one place where both predator and prey must go is the water hole. There, the prey animals sense what distance they must maintain from their enemies, such as lions (10-13). In tall grass, a hungry lioness can hide and creep up on an animal, sometimes striking it down. Since most animals can outrun them, however, lions do not always capture prey easily. Instead, they may steal another animal's meat.

Lions, the largest members of the cat family living in Africa, are the only cats that live in permanent groups. A typical sight on the savanna is a pride of 15 or so lions lying in the shade. Often they rest 20 hours a day, hunting in the early morning and late evening. Lions signal their presence by roaring.

Male ostriches (13-15) make a noise similar to a lion's roar while defend-ing their territory or courting. Often a hissing sound accompanies the roar. Height and exceptional eyesight enable ostriches to spot danger approaching from far away. Zebras often forage close to them. When the ostriches take off—at speeds up to 40 miles an hour—the zebras, too, seek safety.

Heights of up to 19 feet and excellent distance vision help giraffes (27-29) protect themselves. These animals can run at speeds of 35 miles an hour for a short way. Since no other creature on earth is as tall, giraffes have little competition for treetop leaves. The thorny acacias that grow on the savannas provide much of their food. The animals tend to avoid thorns that are large enough to prick them. To reach the high branches, giraffes rely on their long tongues, which can measure up to 21 inches.

A giraffe's spots help camouflage it while it stands among the trees. Its long legs may look like tree trunks, and the spots resemble dappled light. Giraffes spend most of their lives standing. A female does not even lie down to give birth. Her baby may drop more than five feet to the ground without being harmed.

In a special way, giraffes and other giants benefit from some of nature's small creatures. Birds such as oxpeckers and egrets (24) remove insects from the hides of some large animals. While hippos are submerged, fish may help clean their skins, too. In turn, the large animals may churn up food for the smaller ones. This kind of relationship between different animals that live together is known as symbiosis.

While you and your child may not be able to visit these unusual animals in Africa, you can learn more about some of them at a zoo. Next time you go to the zoo with your child, ob-serve elephants, giraffes, ostriches, and other giants as they eat, sleep, and move around. Discuss your discoveries. You may notice, for instance, that a hippo's eyes, ears, and nose are high on its head. This enables the hippo to keep almost its entire body underwater.

Here are more activities your children might enjoy:
• Make up a story about two lions drinking at a water hole. What other animals are nearby? How long will they have to wait to get a drink? What will happen if the lions suddenly move?

• Not all the animals living in Africa are big. At a library, you can find books on the many other creatures that share the grasslands and mountains with elephants, hippos, and gorillas. Look for information about zebras and other animals that live in herds; flamingos and other birds; reptiles; and insects. Explore how these animals survive.

ADDITIONAL READING

Animals of the Grasslands, by Sylvia A. Johnson. (Minneapolis, Lerner Publications Company, 1976). Ages 8 and up.

Book of Mammals, 2 vols., (Washington, D.C., National Geographic Society, 1981). Ages 8 and up.

Giraffes, by Cathy Kilpatrick. (Milwaukee, Raintree Childrens Books, 1980). Ages 8-12.

Gorillas, by Anthony Wootton. (East Sussex, Wayland Publishers Limited, 1981). Ages 8-12.

Hippos, by C. H. Trevisick. (Milwaukee, Raintree Childrens Books, 1980). Ages 8-12.

How Animals Behave: A New Look at Wildlife. (Washington, D.C., National Geographic Society, 1984). Ages 8-12.